Emotional Choice

To order additional copies, please contact us.
BookSurge, LLC
www.booksurge.com
I-866-308-6235
orders@booksurge.com

Emotional Choice

Caregivers Surviving
Alzheimer's Disease

Ann Fowler Everett

2005

Emotional Choice

TABLE OF CONTENTS

This book is dedicated to:

George A. Fowler
1925-2004

George's siblings and their spouses:
Branson and Norma,
Gary and Frances,
Betty, and Ann

George's grandchildren,
especially Bryan

My nieces and nephews
who loved George so well,
especially Sarah
who sat at George's death bed

My Mother, Velma

My Editor, Joleen Webb

All the angels in Chapter 5

Bob Everett
who gave me new dreams

FORWARD

Caregiving is the most horrid, exquisite, self-defeating, rewarding period in a person's life. Rage, belly-laughs, fear, joy, hurt, and moments of total satisfaction ride in and out as crashing waves of emotion throughout the day—every day, year after year.

No book on caregiving prepares a person to wear the robe of stress and exhaustion, a weight on the shoulders and binding around the heart. Caregivers may die before the patient. The percentage of caregiver deaths varies depending on the study – from 50% to almost 70%.

Each caregiving experience is different from all others, because loved ones and caregivers come with individual personalities, strengths and vulnerabilities. For this reason, each caregiver becomes an expert on caregiving and on their loved one. No doctor or other authority knows more about the loved one than the caregiver.

I was a caregiver for 17 years, from the first signs of Alzheimer's to George's death at home. I wish I would have known more about protecting myself from excessive moving, from my pain as others expressed denial of the disease, and from my own need to do everything myself. I had much to learn.

As I share my story, I want to give caregivers the option of *emotional choice*. The term emotion divorce is frequently used. Because people cringe at the word divorce and associate the word with abandonment, I have chosen to use the phrase *emotional choice*.

Emotional choice gives the caregiver the right to take respite, permission to dream of life after disease, and the freedom to be an advocate for a loved one.

I offer my poems, stories and journaling notes as inspiration for caregivers and friends of caregivers. Caregiver stories are the closest thing we have to road maps.

I hope my story reaches one person in denial. The denial of Alzheimer's is a rejection of the caregiver's reality. Over and over again, I heard other caregiver's talk about denial by children, siblings and friends. Aside from George's decline, for me denial was the most painful part of the process.

More community based organizations and churches need to reach out with meals and respite long before the loved one's final weeks of life. Friends disappear over the caregiving years and isolation builds walls of despair.

George gave me his greatest gifts during the last decade of our thirty year marriage. Surely life provides no better school for personal growth. Caregiving is unconditional love even when the conditions are painful and smelly. Caregiving is learning who you are at the core — a place far beyond the mumblings of pulpit quotes or trite words from greeting cards. Caregiving is a privilege; and like all sacrifices on life's battlefields, there is a price to be paid.

CHAPTER ONE

Searching for Home

THE CARETAKER

If I, the poet, could form sentences
to separate my life from his,
place disjointed lessons in stanzas
or make something beautiful of pain,
then I could begin to find
who I have become during his dying,
the dying process of yesterday and tomorrow.
Today...........unspeakable.

The monster, Alzheimer's,
slithered lazily into our home,
sat unfed during the long winter,
watched his victim through half-closed eyes,
stroked his fears with his tongue.
The delusions began.
Memory lessened.
My love inched away from me
and sat on the monster's back.

Then the feeding. Slowly at first.
I saw him slip inside the monster's jaws.
I screamed, "Do not leave me."

He told monster tales —
his parents sleeping in our home,
the return of children
and voices speaking from empty rooms.

I watched him struggle
against the monster's clenched jaws,
the possession complete, death so far away.
Swallowed whole, his bulk swelled
the belly of the disease.

I was left with the creature.

Something in the creature's smile
reminded me of a man who fed squirrels,
rode free on a motorbike
through Florida orange groves,
knew the forest trees by name,
studied the stars, made love to me
and to the whole of his existence.
So I stayed. I listened for his laugh.

I cared for the disease,
loved and stroked the lump
which represented my husband,
I tended the pain and endured the ranting.
I laid beside the monster at night and
awakened to confusion
in the wee hours of the morning.

I forgot who I am.
Surely this is so,

because I once knew words.
Words are who I am.
Ann Everett 2002

TRYING TO FIND THE PERFECT HOME

The first signs of Alzheimer's may not be memory loss, but rather a lack of logic, an overwhelming feeling when faced with day to day chores, or inappropriate responses to stress when driving or spending time with family.

George and I sold our north Georgia home in 1982 and traveled full time in a thirty-five foot Avion Travel Trailer. In 1987 George began to exhibit irrational behavior. For example he insisted we stop on a hill while he walked to the top to see if the road continued. I was left to direct traffic on two-lane roads. At that point I insisted the trailer be sold.

I took George to a young doctor in Florida and described the symptoms. He asked George to give his mother's maiden name and had him count backwards by threes from twenty-two. He passed with flying colors. The Doctor looked at me as if I were demented and gave a knowing look to George.

I had the same reaction to my suspicions from his sons and friends. So I became silent about his diminished capacity. I entered caregiver's isolation.

We had a home built in an Orlando suburb. I thought it would be perfect for George, two golf courses in the subdivision and a zero lot line. Within two years the rural feel was gone. A strip mall popped up two blocks from our house and a four-lane to Disney backed up to our property line.

George was becoming more agitated in traffic. He exhibited road rage, one time continuing to dart in and out with another driver for over two miles in heavy traffic. I never again allowed George to drive in city traffic. I became more assertive.

George wanted nothing more than to move from Orlando. We looked at housing in my home town of Hope, Kansas. No traffic. No Disney World. Little stress. He could drive comfortably to a nearby golf course.

We bought a lovely home on three lots. Within a few years, he was overwhelmed by upkeep and refused to allow anyone else do yard work. I did not make the *emotional choice* to be assertive and insist on keeping my home. This was a mistake.

We moved to a Herington apartment in the same town as the golf course. Then moved to another apartment. Too hot. Too cold. Too whatever.

We bought another home in Herington. Small house on a small lot.

After a few years, I would be the one to choose to move for the benefit of hospice. *Emotional choice.* Best for him. Best for me. A sign of my personal growth.

WHAT NO ONE TELLS YOU ABOUT ALZHEIMERS

1. Alzheimer's is more than memory loss. Logic and appropriate behavior will be lost.
2. People with Alzheimer's are great at covering up their losses with good social behavior, such as camaraderie on the golf course and coffee with the guys at the local drug store.
3. Physicians do not necessarily know how to diagnose Alzheimer's. Although the MMSE serves a purpose midway into the disease, it does not reflect the many earlier changes.
4. Denial by family and friends is commonplace and hurtful.
5. People with Alzheimer's change jobs more often, or in

George's case move more frequently, than the general population.

EMOTIONAL CHOICE

In the beginning I was uncertain of my caregiver role. More than anything, I wanted George to enjoy his remaining years and was willing to make sacrifices for his comfort.

The frequent moves were emotionally, as well as financially, expensive. I now know I could have made a better choice by moving directly from the Avion Travel Trailer to rural Kansas and insisted we hire help to remain in one home. Because of his distress, I was not secure enough to make that choice.

Why did I not assert my feelings? I needed to take the first step towards emotional choice by distancing myself from the hysteria of his position.

Choosing sound financial planning in regards to our property would not have been selfish or poor caregiving. George's neediness was not going to be solved by any move. He was slipping away from me by inches, and I was slipping with him, a second victim of the disease.

CHAPTER TWO

Embracing Grief

I NEEDED TO GRIEVE WHEN:

- **I left George in Nursing Home Daycare for the first time.** The process of approval required two visits with social workers, paperwork, and doctor's orders. I cried for over thirty minutes after I left him. (July 2002)

- **Conversation with an Intelligent Man became Impossible.** Conversations in 2002 went something like this:

  "George, you need to change your shirt for your doctor's appointment."

  George replied, "Where is my shirt?"

  "In your closet," I said calmly.

  George asked, "Where's my closet?"

  I directed him to the bedroom and he asked, "What am I looking for?"

  Then we repeated the entire conversation.

- **I SAW HIM LOSING THE ABILITY TO PARTNER.** George loved to help around the house, especially after his world became so small. One day in August 2002 I asked him to make the bed. He forgot the top sheet and pillowcases.

- **HE HURT UNNECESSARILY.** George was convinced people were angry with him. For instance, we drove to Salina and the entire day he believed he had left his brothers, Branson and Gary, at the house. Fascinating how people with dementia can remember the wrong idea all day but not receive and remember correct information.

- **I GAVE UP MY JOB TO STAY HOME WITH GEORGE.** My full time job was a volunteer effort. I co-founded The Family Resource Exchange, a welfare-to-work organization, and loved working with families. The time came when George needed round-the-clock supervision. I could not afford to pay for care and give my time away. I knew I could give more loving care than outsiders.

- **HE COULD NO LONGER REMEMBER HOLIDAYS.** In February 2003 the Herington Nursing Home invited George and me to their Valentine's Dinner. They had George make a valentine and give me a flower. The tablecloth was bright red dotted with white hearts. Candles were lit and the lights lowered. This was a positive way to grieve and give passage to a change in our relationship.

- **HE COULD NOT COMPLETE A CHILD'S PUZZLE.** In an effort to provide activity for George, I bought him a 25-piece, ages 3-7, puzzle. I envisioned sitting at the table with him and discussing holidays and family as we put the puzzle together. Because I did not want to insult him, I told him we were putting the puzzles together to see if they were too difficult for grandbabies. He did not respond negatively to the simplistic pictures as he fingered the pieces. I laid a corner piece close to where it should be placed. George could not make it fit and could no longer grasp the puzzle concept. (September 2003)

- **FAMILY AND FRIENDS WERE IN DENIAL ABOUT HIS ILLNESS.** Other than the loss of a loved one, denial is the most painful part of this process. People who deny their parent, sibling or friend has Alzheimer's also deny the caregiver's reality. Because family will remain part of the caregiver's life, a place in the heart must be found for people who cause hurt during the caregiving experience.
- **I FAILED TO BE PATIENT.** I expected my perfect performance in a situation far from perfect.

GRIEF

Good emotional choices will be based on the ability to grieve. Grief is not solely an after-the-death experience for the caregiver. Grief gets a daily workout. Emotional choice is the door beyond grief.

Big losses are taking the car keys away, hiring a caregiver, or placing a loved one in adult pull-ups. Caregivers expect the big changes. Because others can identify with the pain associated with obvious declines, grieving big losses may be easier than small changes sapping energy and discouraging caregivers.

Small erosions remind us the caregiver is absolutely alone with the decisions, responsibilities, and survival of the caregiver's own emotional health. Small changes require processing every day.

Caregivers can not spend energy feeling pity for the loved one, anger when the loved one hurls hurtful words, frustration over the spilled milk, hopelessness with the futility of treatment. The grief would be overwhelming. All energy is needed for caregiving.

The answer is two-fold: 1) make the emotional choice to distance yourself from the loved one's reality so you can continue to function as caregiver and advocate; and 2) grieve each loss and let it go for emotional stability.

Alzheimer's can not be fixed. Grieve the diagnosis and decide whether you are capable of being a caregiver. Can you lose sleep? Are you willing to have respite providers in your home? Are you strong enough to be an advocate for your loved one with physicians, family members in denial and respite providers who will undermine your confidence? Are you in good health? Do you have a sense of humor? Are you willing to do your grief work?

If you enlist as a caregiver, steel yourself for unconditional love. The adult you love will disappear and a child will fill your days.

Grief is an individual experience. I grieve in a variety of ways — humor, tears, hugs, sharing with others. Find ways to grieve the movement from one Alzheimer's stage to another and name it grief. Then look for the positives in the new stage of the disease.

A friend of mine, Joanie, had calling cards printed to share with people who were confronted by her husband. The cards simply thanked the waitress, store clerk, or other unsuspecting public person for their patience with her husband who had Alzheimer's Disease. I also had cards printed to slip to people who were confused or angered by George's behavior. Amazing how this simple practice made angels out of angry humans. The cards opened doors of understanding for both George and the person who held the card.

The last month of George's life he crawled on the floor and played with toys and stuffed animals. Nursing homes would have drugged him, my sweet baby, and strapped him in a chair. He was a loving person of value, just as important as when he was a professional man held in esteem by his peers. He had love, smiles and hugs to give. What more can a person ask from another human being? This would be my last loss to grieve.

One thing I did not grieve was regret.

WHAT NO ONE TELLS YOU ABOUT ALZHEIMER'S

I.   Alzheimer's is a family disease. Everyone is affected, even those in denial who do not know unconditional love and are incapable of healthy grief.

2.   Alzheimer's is going backwards on the developmental chart – adult to child. The better this is understood, the easier it is to accept and embrace the loved one.

3.   The healthiest caregivers distance themselves from the love one's negative remarks under the influence of the disease. A familiar phrase to caregivers is, "It is the disease, not the person."

4.   Caregivers must grieve every loss. Processing caregiver feelings rather than keeping pain bound inside the chest translates into emotional and physical survival.

EMOTIONAL CHOICE

I.   Choose to either give unconditional love or make other arrangements for your loved one. Consider the caregiver's physical and emotional health before making a final decision.

2.   Choose to laugh.

3.   Choose to do deliberate grief work regarding the death process.

4.   Choose to grieve for family members in denial. If dealing with other's denial is too costly for the caregiver, find someone else in the family or a friend to communicate directly with them. I found family letters convenient. You must not allow those in denial to sap your emotional energy.

5.   Accept reality.

6.   Choose to dream of "someday" rather than live in the past or find yourself overwhelmed with the present.

CHAPTER THREE

Laugh Rather Than Cry

HUMOR FROM MY JOURNAL

Dressing for Church

George had special challenges dressing. He could not put both arms in his shirt without bringing the remainder of the shirt up behind his neck. I always helped him pull down the back of his shirt and get the buttons matched up. One morning I was at my computer when George arrived in his usual disarray. One shirt sleeve hung below his knuckles and the other was almost up to his elbow. He looked at me and said, "I can't wear this to church, one sleeve is longer than the other." (2002)

The Traffic Stop

The last time George drove, he was stopped by a sheriff's deputy because he went through a four-way stop. When asked why he did not stop, George said, "If everyone stopped, how would anyone get anywhere?" George received a warning. (2002)

Pick up the Trash

On trash pickup day, I had George gather and empty all the waste baskets. One day I said, "George gather up all the trash around the house." He smiled and left to complete the chore. I soon realized he was not in the house. I found him outside. He said, "I can't find any trash around the house." (2002)

Help!

Hospice was in place and the aide, Villa, came for her first visit. Her primary job was to help George bathe. George was still mobile. With the aide's assistance, he was ready for a shower. While she started the water, he pulled his pants back on. She patiently removed his pants and he pulled them back on and up, again and again. George escaped, holding on to his pants, and scooting up the stairs. He was naked, except for his pants hanging below his buttocks, and screaming, "She is trying to kill me! She is trying to kill me!" Villa became George's best friend and treated him with respect until his death. (2003)

George's Second Wife

With the help of my Dentist, Dr. Harlan Boyce, and his staff, George's dental hygiene and general oral health was maintained. Kendra was the sweet hygienist who chased George down repeatedly after he escaped from the chair and patiently cleaned his teeth. George was quite fond of her. As we left the dentist's office one day, he proudly said, "She is my other wife." (2003)

Try to Win an Argument with an Alzheimer's Victim

George attended a district church meeting with me regarding homosexuality and the church. A minister and four of his angry flock sat at our table. George wanted to win the argument of inclusion so he said, "Where was God while the boys were dying in WWII?" The participants' confusion tickled me. He always carried himself with dignity so people respected his opinions even when they made no sense or were off topic. (1998)

Fly Away Bird

A male cardinal flew into our garage window. Stunned he could not fly. George, tears in his eyes, carried the bird into the house. We took the bird into the backyard and urged him to fly away. George was inconsolable, so we put the bird in the cat carrier and drove to the vet's. The veterinarian did not ordinarily treat birds, but he agreed to keep him if we would purchase bird seed, which we did. The next day the cardinal was fine and released by the vet. We spotted the cardinal in our backyard with his mate. George was happy. (2001)

How Many Smoke Detectors?

George installed two smoke detectors within 8 feet of each other while I was out of the house. When I burned something in the kitchen, both detectors screamed at me. (2001)

Wire Not

While I was gone one afternoon, George rewired switches to the basement. The switches that turned on one set of lights now turned on a new set. He remembered perfectly how to wire, but no longer had reasoning power. A do-it-yourselfer must DO something even in dementia. (2000)

Label Not

George could never remember which of the three switches by the garage door turned on the light he wanted. He decided to label the switches with a red, permanent marker. By the time he turned on a light and identified it, he had forgotten which switch was responsible. All were labeled wrong. We sold the house with the bright red marker labeling. (2000)

Subtract Years

George figured and figured with a pencil and pad until he discovered his age. 1925 to 1995 is seventy years. He did not know the present year. (2002)

Cucumber Madness

Someone gave me cucumbers. George carried them in from the car and they were never seen again. I turned the house upside down looking for them. George must have been a magician. (August 2002)

WHAT NO ONE TELLS YOU ABOUT ALZHEIMER'S
1. Laughter is permissible.
2. Laughter is loving the whole person in a moment totally out of your control.

EMOTIONAL CHOICE
1. Laugh with your loved one.
2. Laugh at yourself in the serendipity of your days.
3. Laugh with friends away from your loved one.
4. Chose a belly laugh every day over negative emotions.

CHAPTER FOUR

Respite

COULD I HAVE THIS DANCE?

George was hospitalized at Abilene's Rose Unit in May 2003.

Each day I sat on the living room sofa and visited a picture of George and me dancing. The photo was taken at his retirement party in 1980. We were not aware the photo had been taken until it arrived in the mail weeks after the party.

I shared this story with Margaret who worked at the Rose Unit. I described the photo, the gaze into one another's eyes and obvious affection between us. I added, "George used to pull me off the sofa and into his arms for a twirl around the living room whenever he heard Ann Murray's song, *Could I Have This Dance.*"

Margaret began to sing, "Could I have this dance for the rest of my life?......"

George, who no longer remembered anniversaries or sometimes even my name, began to sway to the sound of Margaret's lovely voice. In that moment, in a butter yellow hallway, our wedding vows were renewed.

RESPITE

The decision to no longer trust your loved one at home alone is difficult.

My earliest caregiving system did not involve a person but rather notes left on the kitchen counter for George. Later I placed notes in his shirt pockets so he could retrieve them at any time and see where I was and when I would be home. The system worked well for about a year.

In January 2002, I had an out-of-town meeting. Because I knew George could no longer be alone overnight, I took him with me. With a note in his pocket and television to view, he would be fine in the motel room. I called him every thirty minutes for my peace of mind. He was quite content until after checkout.

After lunch George refused to wait a couple hours in the library at my meeting place. George insisted he would walk around Wal-Mart. I wrote a note for his pocket: *Ann will meet you at the Wal-Mart restaurant at the back of the store at 2:30 p.m.*

I was back at 2:30 p.m. and he was no where to be found. I looked up and down every isle. Finally, I asked for help from customer service. They paged him. No response. Second and third pages followed. I was frantic and ready to call the police. Then I spotted him outside the door.

George had been watching for my return in the parking lot. I had let him down. I was determined he would never feel abandoned in a strange place again.

On our drive home George had his last lucid moment. He

said, "It must be hard to be married to someone who can not remember things."

I responded, "I'll never leave you. It will be okay." As I began to elaborate, he slipped back into dementia, never to return as a rational, caring person.

George's first caregiver was Velda, a lady who would sit with him at home when I had meetings or a bridge game. She assumed responsibility for his bathing and engaged him in conversation.

In those years, I was the Herington United Methodist church organist and choir director. When George could no longer sit alone, I took him up front with me. He sat in a chair by the organ. If mid-song he began to wander, Velda or another church member would follow him out of the church and return him to my side. Later, Velda would take him to the seat she shared with her husband. George loved to go to church because he was still social, even after he did not know who people were. They knew him and he felt loved. The congregation became his collective caregiver.

Institutional respite for a couple days was always a challenge. The small Herington Nursing Home was very accommodating and patient with George. The Rose Unit at the Abilene Hospital was exceptional. These experiences were positive.

When the disease progressed, Nursing Homes beyond the small towns of Herington and Abilene attempted to undermine my confidence as a caregiver. They wanted him for their census. They used drugs rather than individual attention to control George's behavior. Finding institutional respite care in the city was very difficult.

At home, under my care, George took few medications for behavior control. He wandered about the house, played with his toys when his mental decline made him childlike, and he enjoyed his support system of family and caregivers. With fewer medications, there were fewer falls and no wheel chair restraints.

Many caregivers must use nursing homes for the care of their loved ones. I highly recommend a nursing home with an Alzheimer's unit. Most of all, a caregiver must visit the loved one. Nursing homes will do a better job with your loved one if a family representative is in and out. Watch for increased stress, odor or bruising. Hold nursing homes responsible for their performances.

Our final experience with caregivers was Total Homecare and Hospice, Wichita, Kansas. I can not begin to recount the many positive and loving ways they cared for George and for me. They have my undying respect and appreciation.

WHAT NO ONE TELLS YOU ABOUT ALZHEIMER'S

1. Social interaction is important if the loved one was social before the disease.
2. The safest place for a loved one is not necessarily the nursing home.
3. Caregivers can be a whole community – church to hospice.

EMOTIONAL CHOICE

1. Choose a respite provider who does not add to caregiver stress.
2. Build a support system in the community, if possible. Keeping your loved one in the larger community is better for both of you. Isolation is unhealthy.
3. All caregivers must have respite. Walking away to refresh yourself is better for you and for your loved one. Loved ones are overly sensitive to love, stress, anger, and all caregiver emotions. Loved ones often misin-

terpret the caregiver's emotional state or weariness and act out in undesirable ways.

4. Make an emotional choice to be healthy. Caregivers who experience respite, eat good foods and have social interactions are more loving and compassionate.

CHAPTER FIVE

Angels

Written in April 2002

I snuggle closer to my husband and feel the definition of his bulk in a knit cap, socks, long johns and flannel pajamas. The heat is on seventy. I sweat from pores surely reinvented to accommodate the needs of a drenched, Alzheimer's caregiver.

George asks, "Where are they going to sleep tonight?"

"Who?"

"The people in the living room?"

"You, the cat and I will sleep in this bed. They can fend for themselves." I rub his chest and kiss his chin.

Satisfied, George drifts into sleep.

Wide awake I entertain the presences only he can see and hear.

I imagine Mary, a former homeowner, strolls about my home. She looks for what is familiar and judges the changes in décor. I wonder if she likes HER home with the interior doors removed — air and guests free to circulate. Mary would never have kept an almost empty refrigerator, bottles of condiments and butter in the door, sour milk and two pitchers of tea on the upper shelf and a half dozen ancient eggs, two of them cracked, on the lowest shelf. How would Mary have begun to prepare gourmet dishes from the cookbook she authored? Convenience foods and sweets fill my freezer. Mary, the ghost, comforts George, sympathetic to a man who receives love expressed in ways not consumed at the table and digested into the wee hours of the morning.

Other nights I imagine George welcomes family members, loved ones who wait for him to complete this long, death process. His brothers, sisters, children and grandchildren share memory space with previous Fowler generations. His mother prepares biscuits in a bread tray. His father tells a joke and runs his fingers across his head as if hair still grew there. Brothers and sisters share stories from their childhood. Children race around the baseball diamond and slide through orange tubes at fast food restaurants. The voices are a surreal mix of all George has ever known.

Recently, I have begun to imagine the voices are the soft comfort of angels. He hears angels when he can not process his sister's words, "I love you, brother." His angels speak in more familiar tones than his sons and brothers. He remembers those mysterious presences but not how we celebrated his birthday. I wonder if "death angels" are all that is real and life is the illusion. At life's end, do we return to what we knew before conception? Maybe in his forgetfulness, he finds wisdom we have yet to learn.

Before I roll from George's side and take my sleep position, I thank Mary, his family and the angels for caring enough to visit. May they have a peaceful night and help us through another day.

THE SPIRITUAL JOURNEY

Regardless the belief system, a compassionate person can not complete the caregiver's journey unchanged. I define a spiritual experience as any moment that changes the heart. Soul, created from pain, is the reward after the loved one's bed is emptied and the pill bottles have been tossed.

I met some special angels along the way, more than I can recount here.

Family

- George's siblings and their spouses were always supportive. Wonderful in-laws.
- My niece, Sarah, stayed with me the last week of George's life. She also traveled to Georgia for George's memorial service. Remarkable woman!
- Grandson Bryan called his grandfather and remembered him (and me) with cards. He understood family lineage and had the ability to show affection. Special man!
- My sister and brother-in-law, Diane and Arnold, helped me move and move and move. So patient.
- My Mother visited with me every day by phone.

The Public

- George loved Dwight, a waiter at IHOP. Dwight had a gentle, humorous manner and always lifted my spirits. He talked to George rather than shying away from the diseased man. Dwight respected George's humanity, even when he attempted to exit alarmed doors or wander away from the table. Dwight made a difference each time he touched one of our difficult days.

- The waitress at the Barb's Café in Herington remembered to serve George decaf coffee and always called him by name.

- One day I had severe tooth pain and one hour of hospice respite to find a dentist. The minute the aide arrived, I darted out the door. I had tried numerous dentists listed in the phone book and found no one in the office because of a dental conference. I stopped at the dentist's office closest to my home and found Dr. Harlan Boyce in his shorts cleaning carpet on his day off. The kind man took me in, gave me prescriptions for antibiotics and pain relievers, and made an appointment for the dreaded root canal. Dr. Boyce and his staff are angels. It was the beginning of a positive relationship that would help carry me through caregiving and into my new life. Good people are magic.

- People, whose names I never knew, helped me when I had challenges with George at the grocery store.

People Who Know Alzheimer's

- At 2:30 a.m. kind voices from Alzheimer's Association helped me process my choices.

- My hospice team was extraordinary and heaven sent. Sheri, Kathy, Joyce, Villa and Dr. Penner provided George with dignity until his death.

- Karla, a special nurse who saw the patients as whole people at the Herington Nursing Home, embraced George and sent a beautiful note after his death. Angels, each one of them.

WHAT NO ONE TELLS YOU ABOUT CAREGIVING

1. There are rewards: laughter, satisfaction, growth, new friendships, angels, new skills, knowledge, and wisdom.
2. It is the hardest thing you will ever do.
3. Some people you expect the most from will let you down and strangers will become your angels.
4. Love relationships change – the spouse becomes your child. Love is good however it is defined.
5. Caregivers learn less about Alzheimer's, institutions of care and insurance companies than they learn about themselves.

THE EMOTIONAL CHOICES

1. Look for positives rather than negatives. Go to the restaurant with the caring waiter and do not worry about eating pancakes five times a week.
2. Play, shop and dine out with your loved one as long as you can rather than spend energy cleaning the house.
3. When the loved one can not shop or dine out, the caregiver must continue to play away from home.
4. Accept the change of caring for a spouse to caring for an elderly child. If you expect your spouse to feel your needs, you will be disappointed. If you love any person unconditionally and expect nothing but the pleasure of giving and learning, you will be greatly rewarded.
5. Feed your spirit or perish. You do not need to be religious to have meaningful moments with your loved one, your support system and the community. Be open to delight.

CHAPTER SIX

Widowhood

THE WIDOW (2004)

I am a widow. I am a widow. I am a widow. Saying it three times makes the reality of loss no more real. Perhaps George is more alive in his death than I.

After thirty years of marriage and seventeen years of caregiving, I do not remember who I was before George. Not an admirable or possible goal to become that former self. I am simply too tarnished to create a new self out of memories, the weight gained trying to swallow the pain, the familiar routine.

I returned George to Georgia, to the county of his birth and rearing, to his brothers and sisters, and to parents and grandparents buried near the site of his ashes. The decision was logical and a small thank you to a family who was kind to the end to George and to me.

The memorial was the most beautiful I have ever seen. The bulletins my niece, Sarah, and I put together with old pictures of George engaged guests. The minister's words were tonally pleasing and gracious.

George's niece, Cheryl, sang "Could I Have This Dance" and tears welled in my eyes. I could feel George holding me on the dance floor, looking into my eyes and kissing me on the forehead. My cheeks remained dry.

After a tribute to George's military service and taps, I accepted the perfectly folded flag. When I gave it to his middle son who retired from the navy, he wept. I did not shed a single tear. Everyone said I was a "class act" standing on the treeless hill midst ground level markers and his relatives.

After my return home, the dysfunction of wandering aimlessly in my own house continued day to day. I could not coordinate cleaning the dust I saw. My glasses were lost and later found on my head. I reported lost credit cards and bothered the bank about simple transactions. Sleep came at odd hours, never at night.

I struggled to write acknowledgments. The foreign words spilled into the computer and I was uncertain of sentence structure, any complete thought surely an accident.

I smiled when I opened my bathroom vanity door. One of George's aides decided to reorganize. She was young and looked for ways to help. My bathroom tissue, all 48 rolls, were removed from the original packaging and stacked to form a white wall.

Perhaps with time, when the white wall lowers, I will be able to cry.

THE WHITE WALL

Most long term caregivers are ready for the death of a loved one. The reality of things worse than death is best known by the caregiver. A caregiver knows a loved one never would wish the long death process for themselves or for a caregiver losing sleep, aging too fast, and grieving the many losses.

Over my caregiver years, I talked to hundreds of caregivers in online support chat rooms, following talks I gave on Alzheimer's, in a face-to-face local support group, and in the community. Most caregivers were my heroes. They had much to teach me; and, in time I had my own wisdom to share.

Some of the most interesting caregivers were those in caregiver chat years after the death of a loved one. They were still grieving. Their circular thinking replayed caregiving without resolution. Resentments toward family were vented and the recalling of their weariness retold. The results of long term trauma can be long term healing — or no healing, but long term grieving.

I had done my grief work during George's dying and believed I would avoid grief after his death. I was so wrong. However, my grief was briefer because I had done my emotional choice work throughout his illness. I knew I had another life at the end of our journey together.

When the white wall lowered, I did cry. It was four months after his death and I had been asked to go out on my first date in over thirty years. The day before the date, I started to sob. I had to completely let go of my grief to find new joys.

Far more courage is needed to find happiness than to grieve.

Grief is self-serving, however necessary for some time following death. Grief can be the crutch allowing us time to heal or keep us emotional cripples.

Caregivers know more about love than any theology professor, talk-show host, psychologist, or newly wed. They have experienced unconditional love, the absolutes in giving.

Caregiver bodies may be a bit worn, but the depth of love is boundless and they have much to give after the dying. Those who let go of the grief will rediscover love in unexpected places.

WHAT NO ONE TELLS YOU
ABOUT THE WHITE WALL

1. The fuzzy white wall enveloping us following the death of a loved one can be a pillow for support and cushioning during the healing or it can become a wasted life in the fog.

2. Just as you drive in and out of the fog on a long drive home, so will you have good and bad days on the long drive to emotional wellness.

EMOTIONAL CHOICE

1. Process grief during the dying, not just at the end. Grieve each small loss and then move forward.

2. Choose to accept the fog. Your subconscious mind is working through the pain. Go to a movie or cuddle up with a book. Let the mind do its work while you drink cocoa in the fog.

3. Choose life for yourself. Do not let the loved one's death be your death. You have a life waiting for you.

4. Choose to give your love to someone else. You NEED to love or you would not have been a caregiver. Bake cookies for a grandchild. Volunteer anywhere. Date – oh, so scary!

CHRONOLOGY OF GEORGE'S DISEASE

Each person with Alzheimer's Disease (AD) will create his/her own calendar. Although no two people are alike, a caregiver wants to know other time tables. Not knowing where a loved one is in the process of the disease is frustrating. A caregiver always looks for identifying markers in the stories of others.

1987
- George's first obvious signs of Alzheimer's.
- On the Global Deterioration Scale (GDS), George would be considered at Level 3—Incipient.

1989
- George could no longer handle heavy traffic in Orlando. Following road rage events, we moved to Hope, Kansas to be in a small community and near family.

1995
- George could no longer manage caring for a yard. He was overwhelmed by our three lots, but refused to allow me to hire help. We moved into an apartment.

1996
- On the Global Deterioration Scale, George would be at Level 4 – Mild.

1998
- Our fourth home in eight years was purchased.

1999
- On the Global Deterioration Scale, George is at Level 5 – Moderate.

2000

- What I called my "year of abuse" as George verbally raged against me often and at unexpected times. Very unpredictable.

2001

- Olfactory hallucinations. George smelled gas and other odors in sheets, carpeting, etc. when no odor was present.
- George had difficulty using utensils to cut steak.
- George's last summer to drive to the Golf Course.
- (December) Risperdal dosage was doubled. George hit the cat and tried to access the car.

2002

- George was at Level Six, Moderately Severe, of the Global Deterioration Scale for Degenerative Dementia.
- (January) Exelon was begun. Aricept was no effective for George.
- George began looking for his parents and forgot their deaths.
- George believes the reflection in the bathroom mirror is another man.

2003

- January 3 George was admitted to the Abilene Rose Unit. His medications were adjusted.
- (February) Exelon was stopped because it was not helping him and he had stomach problems.
- Ativan was prescribed "as needed" to help him relax for baths or when frustrated.
- Velda was employed to give him baths and care for him whenever I had to be out of the house.
- George refused to change his clothes. He wanted to wear the same clothing for several days.

- George began sleeping in a hospital bed with the rails up.
- (March) Sold his car and reported his dementia to the DMV.
- (April) The neurologist defined George's illness as "dementia consistent with degenerative-type, i.e., Alzheimer's." Weight loss was evident.
- (June) First Incontinence.
- (June) Heightened confusion. He did not know where he was or who I was at times.
- Began to wander from home and church.
- Placed a Safe Return bracelet on his wrist and notified the local police regarding his challenges with memory.
- Delusions and hallucinations.
- Used nursing home daycare at times in addition to Velda's visits.
- I slept in a recliner from January to August so I could block the bedroom door in case George decided to wander.
- Childproof locks were a necessity in the car. He tried to exit from the back seat.
- George was in adult pull-ups.
- (August) We moved to Wichita because hospice help was refused in Herington. They could not determine how long George would live.
- (August) Hospice began in Wichita.
- (September) George drank glass after glass of soda. He became quite angry when I try to stop him after 5 glasses downed in a matter of a few minutes.
- George forgot where the restroom was and urinated

in inappropriate places. He washed his hands in the toilet and left faucets on throughout the house.

- I had to repeat the same word many times for him to understand. As a rule I used one- or two-word sentences. For instance, "seat belt." I did not say, "Put on your seat belt, George." He could not process lengthy verbiage.
- (November) Rapid decline. George was putting plastic, play letters in his mouth.
- (November) George was violent for the first time. He sprained my wrist and hit me numerous times until the medication was regulated properly.
- I was feeding him small bites of sandwiches and cookies because he could no longer eat from the plate. He did not want to be fed.
- (December) George crawled on the floor.

2004

- George was at level seven of the Global Deterioration Scale.
- Sleep activity increased.
- He would not allow his teeth to be brushed.
- Weight loss was dramatic, six pounds in one week.
- George fell several times.
- George could no longer swallow his medications.
- Actively dying (January 12). He could no longer walk or move from the bed. He did not respond to communication.
- Death (January 19)

EMOTIONAL CHOICE

POEMS BY ANN FOWLER EVERETT

THE GIFT OF NOW
2002 Christmas Poem

A hedge row stitches suede sky to prairie patches.
I brake for a weather red truck
and read the "eat beef" bumper sticker.
My pulse slows as Public Radio plays
Jesu, Joy of Man's Desiring.

'Tis the season of joy and love,
the celebration of birth.
I study a cloud blowing across the sky
and feel the wind pushing my Intrepid;
the inevitability of death is not in season.

The truck stops; turns left.
I return the farmer's wave
and feel the upturn of my mouth.
A smile. Joy. Life.

Soon I will be home with a man
who does not remember past seasons,
when he ate, the date or sometimes my name —
the sum of life in the now.
He would have enjoyed the fast moving cloud.
I regret he is not with me.

I once believed the polish of marriage
was in the memory factory;
each photo lovingly placed in an album
represented a forever reality.
When the now of yesterday is gone,
what do we cherish?

The now embraces each moment as a new birth.
A shared smile captures forever.
A cloud echoes celestial joy.
Holding hands is the all of life.

Wise men (and women) – farmers in red trucks,
men without memory and you, sages all,
celebrate the birth of love in a solitary cloud, a smile,
a touch in the nativity of a moment.

IF ALZHEIMER'S WERE THE WIND
April 2003

Gale force winds ripped through me;
debris lashed the face and bare legs;
dust veiling vision.

Just briefly,
I turned away in defeat,
a moment of respite.

No human dare claim the wind —
the diminished made to bow down,
ruled by the unruly.

I determined I would take a piece of the wind,
own the power, control a stormy minute.
I held open my skirt pocket,
filled gingham with the wind.
The bulge swelled.
Quickly I clamped the pocket to my thigh,
held the wind close.

Behind closed doors, I opened a flattened pocket,
reached inside and fingered a thread,
evidence of a frayed seam.
I dared not look at the thread whipped by the wind.

I wept for the tortured wind,
for the bruise on my thigh,
for frayed seams.

No human dare claim the wind.

CHRISTMAS IS FOR TWO-YEAR-OLDS
Christmas Poem 2003

I live with a two-year-old
who delights with unexpected gifts:
hugs and kisses,
an arm chair sleeve across my shoulder,
dust mitts waving hello from my bed.

His two-year-old mind lives
in a seventy-eight-year-old body -
Christmas less a calendar event
than a return to my loved one's own nativity.

Nativity: Joy in the moment,
Grief unknown,
Peace for the price of an oatmeal cookie.

Two-year-olds reteach these lessons
to wise men/women.
It is what they do best.

Not unlike the Christmas story,
the season for my loved one resonates
protective angels, love, change, joy, and peace.

My wish for you, for the world, this Christmas
is a babe to lead the way
to the crèche of divine humanity.

RECOMMENDED

1) Once I Have Had My Tea, *A Guide To Understanding And Caring For The Memory-Impaired Elderly* by Patricia Hladik, R.N.C.

2) The Caregiver's Bill of Rights by Jo Horne, Author of CareGiving: Helping an Aging Loved One. http://www.zarcrom.com/users/yeartorem/rights.html

3) Safe Return (Information on the Alzheimer's Association Site)

4) Alzheimer's Association National Number I-800-272-3900 www.alz.org In Wichita: Alzheimer's Association of the Great Plains 316-267-7333 or I-800-487-2585

5) Look for Hospice in your local phone directory. My Hospice was INTEGRICARE, INC. D.b.a. Total HomeCare and Hospice, Wichita. 316-945-9797

6) Dr. Barry Reisberg's chart on Functional Stages in Normal Human Development and Alzheimer's Disease http://www.bigtreemurphy.com/Reisberg%20H umn%20Dev.htm